06/19

D0966801

Become a star reader with Caillou!

This three-level reading series is designed for pre-readers or beginning readers and is based on popular Caillou episodes. The books feature common sight words used with limited grammar. Each book also offers a set number of target words. These words are noted in bold print and are presented in a picture dictionary in order to reinforce meaning and expand reading vocabulary.

Level 1
Little Star

For pre-readers to read along
- 125-175 words
- Simple sentences
- Simple vocabulary and common sight words
- Picture dictionary teaching 6 target words

Level 2
Rising Star

For beginning readers to read with support
- 175-250 words
- Longer sentences
- Limited vocabulary and more sight words
- Picture dictionary teaching 8 target words

Level 3
Super Star

For improving readers to read on their own or with support
- 250-350 words
- Longer sentences and more complex grammar
- Varied vocabulary and less-common sight words
- Picture dictionary teaching 10 target words

Text: adaptation by Rebecca Klevberg Moeller
All rights reserved.
Original story written by Sarah Margaret Johanson, based on the animated series CAILLOU
Illustrations: Eric Sévigny, based on the animated series CAILLOU

The PBS KIDS logo is a registered mark of PBS and is used with permission.

Chouette Publishing would like to thank the Government of Canada and SODEC for their financial support.

Books
Tax Credit

Gestion
SODEC

Bibliothèque et Archives nationales du Québec and Library and Archives Canada cataloguing in publication

Moeller, Rebecca Klevberg
Caillou: where is my cat?
(I read with Caillou)
Adaptation of: Caillou: where's Gilbert?
For children aged 3 and up.

ISBN 978-2-89718-342-4

1. Caillou (Fictitious character) - Juvenile literature. 2. Hide-and-seek - Juvenile literature. I. Sévigny, Éric. II. Johanson, Sarah Margaret, 1968- . Caillou: where's Gilbert?. III. Title. IV. Title: Where is my cat?

GV1207.M63 2016   j796.1'4   C2016-940014-X

Printed in China
10 9 8 7 6 5 4 3 2 1   CHO1972 MAY2016

Little Star Level 1

Where is My Cat?

Text: Rebecca Klevberg Moeller, language teaching expert
Illustrations: Eric Sevigny, based on the animated series

ONONDAGA FREE

Caillou plays with Gilbert.

Gilbert is Caillou's **cat**.

Caillou pulls a **toy**.

Gilbert jumps on it.

They are having fun.
They are in the **living room**.

Daddy calls,
"Snack time!"

Caillou says, "Gilbert, stay here!"

His **cat** says,
"Meow! Meow!"

Caillou eats his snack.

He is in the **kitchen**.

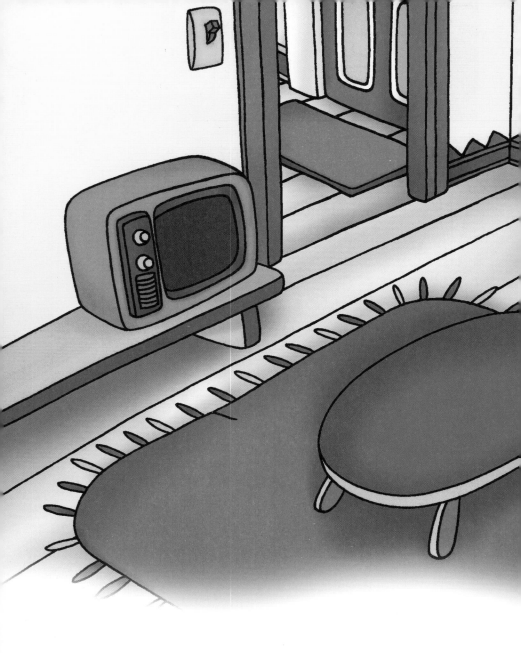

After his snack, Caillou looks for
Gilbert.

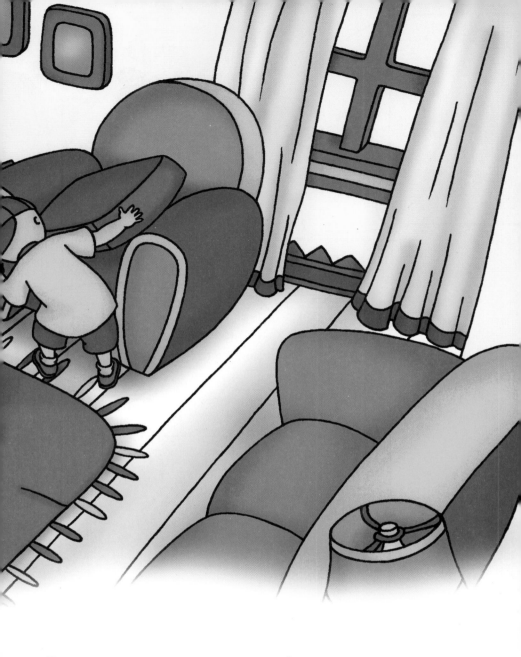

Gilbert is not in the **living room**!

Caillou sees Daddy.
"Where is my **cat**?" he asks.

"He is not in the **kitchen**," Daddy answers.

Caillou sees Mommy.
"Where is my **cat**?" he asks.

"He is not in the **basement**,"
she answers.

Gilbert is not in the **kitchen**.
He is not in the **basement**.

Where is Gilbert?

"Let's look for him," says Mommy.

Is Gilbert in Mommy's **bedroom**?

No **cat** here!

Is Gilbert in Caillou's **bedroom**?

No **cat** here!

Then Caillou sees his **toy**.

"Gilbert?" Caillou calls.

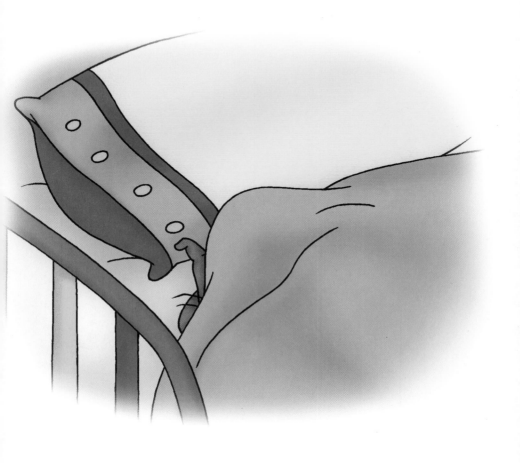

"Meow! Meow!" the **cat** answers.

Caillou looks. His **cat** is in the bed!

Funny Gilbert!

Picture Dictionary

cat

living room

toy

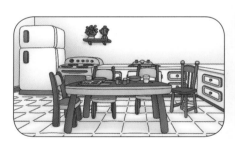

kitchen

basement

bedroom